1939-1945
WORLD WAR TWO

AUTHOR

Luigi Manes (18 July 1966) has already published three books: "The Sherman medium tank in the European theatre of operations" (Soldiershop Publishing, 2019), "Italy 43-45 – AFV's and MV's of co-belligerent units" (Mattioli 1885, 2018) with Paolo Crippa and "Carri armati Sherman in Sicilia" (Edizioni Ardite, 2018) with Lorenzo Bovi. He has written various articles, both for the military modeling magazine "Steel Art" and the website "ModellismoPiù". Always interested in the history of the Second World War, he has a great passion for the Sherman medium tank from an historical and technological point of view.

AUTORE

Luigi Manes (18 luglio 1966) ha già pubblicato tre volumi: "Il carro armato Sherman nel teatro bellico europeo" (Soldiershop Publishing, 2019), "Italia 43-45 – I mezzi delle unità cobelligeranti" (Mattioli 1885, 2018) con Paolo Crippa e "Carri armati Sherman in Sicilia" (Edizioni Ardite, 2018) con Lorenzo Bovi. Ha inoltre realizzato vari articoli per la rivista di modellismo militare "Steel Art" e per il sito "ModellismoPiù". Da sempre interessato alla storia della Seconda Guerra Mondiale, nutre una grande passione per il carro armato medio Sherman, sia dal punto di vista storico sia da quello tecnologico.

For a complete list of Soldiershop titles please contact Luca Cristini Editore on our website: www.soldiershop.com or www.cristinieditore.com. E-mail: info@soldiershop.com

Titolo: **BRITISH TRACKED CARRIERS OF WORLD WAR TWO** Code.: **WTW-006 ENG**
by Luigi Manes.
ISBN code: 978-88-93275026 First edition December 2019
Text: English Nr. di immagini: 151 dimensione: 177,8x254mm Cover & Art Design: Luca S. Cristini

WITNESS TO WAR (SOLDIERSHOP) is a trademark of Luca Cristini Editore, via Orio, 35/4 - 24050 Zanica (BG) ITALY.

WITNESS TO WAR

BRITISH TRACKED CARRIERS OF WORLD WAR TWO

PHOTOS & IMAGES FROM WORLD WARTIME ARCHIVES

LUIGI MANES

SOLDIERSHOP PUBLISHING

BOOKS TO COLLECT

CONTENTS

BRITISH TRACKED CARRIERS OF WORLD WAR TWO

One of the most recognizable tracked vehicles of World War Two was the British Carrier. There were in fact many varieties of this ubiquitous little machine, stemming from the tankettes of the pre-war years. The Carrier was really a spin-off from the development work done on the Dragon Light Gun Tractor by Vickers-Armstrong which built a prototype that could not only tow artillery pieces but also carry a machine gun and its crew. Primarily intended to transport the infantry's support weapons, Carriers were also used as reconnaissance vehicles, armoured observation posts and anti-tank gun tractors.

INITIAL DEVELOPMENT

After the Great War came the need to improve the mobility of the infantry and to help get heavier weapons such as mortars and machine guns to the battlefield. In Great Britain, the first practical step was in 1925, when Major Giffard Le Quesne Martel built a one-man tankette from different parts at his own expense and demonstrated it to the War Office. After a successful test, both Morris Motors and Crossley were authorized to produce one and two-man versions of the home-made vehicle. At the same time, a separate effort was made by Captain John V. Carden who built an unarmoured one-man track-laying vehicle powered by a Ford Model T engine. In the early 1920s, Carden joined Vivian G. Loyd in the management of a large London garage and established with him the firm Carden-Loyd Tractors in Chertsey, working on light tracked vehicles for military use. The last model of Carden-Loyd tankettes was the MK VI which appeared in 1928, in the same year that the firm was taken over by Vickers-Armstrong. Although basically a machine gun carrier, the Carden-Loyd MK VI was also adapted to carry mortars, smoke-projectors and to tow artilleries. Built in significant numbers, this little vehicle gave way to two different lines of development, the light tanks and the light artillery tractors. The tracked gun tractors, also known as Dragons (Dragon was the corruption of the term 'drag gun' which indicates the primary role of these vehicles), were designed to tow an artillery piece with its ammunition limber and to carry a gun crew. The prototype of the Dragon MK III was fitted with a Ford V8 engine which drove the back axle and adopted a steering wheel which activated a sliding cross tube connecting the foremost suspension units on each side. When the steering wheel was turned to the right or to the left, the sliding shaft displaced both front bogies sideways, warping the tracks and causing the vehicle to make a gradual steer. Sharp steering was achieved by turning the wheel hard, an action that would brake the rear drive sprocket to one side or the other. With the exception of the Loyd and T16 Carriers, all subsequent models were built with this ingenious steering mechanism. In 1934, Vickers-Armstrong produced a new prototype designated VA D50 (Vickers-Armstrong Dragon 50) that could be used either to tow artillery pieces or to carry a

Vickers machine gun. The vehicle was equipped with the same type of Horstmann suspension bogies used on the latest Dragon Light Gun Tractors. A right-hand drive experimental Armoured Machine Gun Carrier derived directly from the VA D50 was used as a basis for a subsequent prototype termed as 'General Scout Vehicle', armed with a Bren light machine gun and a Boys anti-tank rifle. In April 1936, Vickers-Armstrong was contracted for 13 machines of what was known as Armoured Machine Gun Carrier No 1 MK I. Some of the No 1 MK Is were modified for different roles. One of them resulted in an improved variant, the Armoured Machine Gun Carrier No 2 MK I which introduced an enlarged gunner's compartment that was extended forward and housed a Vickers medium machine gun. The companies involved in the production of these Carriers were Vickers- Armstrong, Sentinel Waggon, Nuffield, Aveling-Barford and Thornycroft. In 1937, Vickers-Armstrong converted one Armoured Machine Gun Carrier into another prototype, the Cavalry Carrier, a vehicle intended to carry 8 men and tow a gun. Nuffield built 50 Cavalry Carriers and some were employed in France by the British Expeditionary Force in 1940.

▼ A Morris-Martel two-man tankette. Private collection

▲ The Carden-Loyd two-man tankette armed with a Lewis Gun. Private collection

▼ One of the most famous armoured vehicles of the inter-war period was the Carden-Loyd MK VI. This tankette carries a Vickers machine gun. Private collection

▲ A Light Dragon MK IIC. A number of these gun tractors were shipped out to France and served with the Royal Horse Artillery in 1940. Author's collection

▼ A Light Dragon MK III. Some MK IIIs went to France with the British Expeditionary Corps. The majority of these vehicles were either destroyed or abandoned in the retreat. Private collection

▲ The VA D50 (Vickers-Armstrong Dragon 50) fitted with a Vickers machine gun. Author's collection

▼ A unique picture of the Machine Gun Carrier modified into a 'General Scout Vehicle'. Australian War Memorial

▲ An Armoured Machine Gun Carrier No 1 MK I with the Vickers machine gun in position. This vehicle had large armoured lamps on the front. Note the low-positioned front idler wheel. Private collection

▼ The Armoured Machine Gun Carrier No 2 MK I with its redesigned front superstructure. It seems that one of these machines have served with the British Expeditionary Force in 1940. Author's collection

▲ This picture shows the prototype Cavalry Carrier. Private collection

THE BREN CARRIER

In 1935, a light machine gun based upon a Czech design and called the Bren, was introduced in the British Army. From 1937 onwards, the old Machine Gun Carrier was adapted to transport the new weapon. In this respect, Vickers-Armstrong built a prototype vehicle with an hull made of mild steel, named the Bren No 1 MK I Carrier, strictly based on the Armoured Machine Gun Carrier. Thornycroft was the first manufacturer to produce Bren No 2 MK I Carriers. In this case an earlier contract for Armoured Machine Gun Carriers was altered in favour of the Bren Carrier. The Bren No 2 MK I, fitted with a 79E Ford V8 engine, was essentially a Carrier to be used in support of the infantry. This tracked vehicle made its combat debut in northwestern Europe in 1940. Even if the gunner was able to fire the Bren from the vehicle, under normal circumstances the weapon crew should dismount and open fire, permitting the Carrier to withdraw to a safer place. A number of Bren Carriers were also equipped with a Boys anti-tank rifle. The Bren No 2 MK II Carrier was powered by a 79F Ford V8 engine which had American electrical equipment.

▲ Front three-quarter view of a Bren Carrier No 2 MK I. The front idler wheel is now mounted higher. The vehicle has a civil registration plate (HMH 209). Author's collection

▼ Three-quarter rear view of the Bren Carrier with civil registration plate HMH 209. The track adjusting tool (also known as the 'shepherd's crook'), carried on the left side and the typical rear folding flap can be seen clearly. Author's collection

▲ British Bren Carriers on the Brussels-Louvain road (Belgium, 12 May 1940). These vehicles carried a white square on their hull front, sides and rear as a general recognition mark. Private collection

▼ A Bren Carrier captured by Italian troops. Lafaruk (Somaliland), September 1940. Private collection

▲ A Bren Carrier manned by Australian troops. The census number, T 2982, suggests that this is likely to be a vehicle of a batch regarding an earlier contract for Machine Gun Carriers No 2 Mk I, altered in favour of the Bren Carrier. Egypt, October 1940. Australian War Memorial

▼ An Australian Bren Carrier pictured near Beit Jiria (Palestine), in July 1941. Note the Bren machine gun protruding from the gunner's firing slot and the Boys anti-tank rifle above the crew's heads. Australian War Memorial

THE SCOUT CARRIER

An Armoured Machine Gun Carrier was reworked as pilot model for the Scout Carrier, a reconnaissance fighting vehicle equipped with a No 11 Wireless Set and armed with a Bren light machine gun and a Boys anti-tank rifle. Production machines had a reversed built-up rear superstructure. The radio compartment was placed behind the driver, on the right side of the engine and was protected by armour. The majority of these Carriers saw service in France with the British Expeditionary Force but a few were destined for North Africa. Production of the Scout Carrier ended in January 1940.

▲ The Scout Carrier prototype (T 1834). Private collection

▼ ANNABELLA, a disabled Scout Carrier believed to be from 1st British Armored Division. France, Spring 1940. US NARA

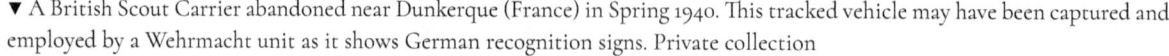

▲ A British Scout Carrier MK I moves forward on a French road. The rear section of the armour protecting the radio compartment with its hinged flap folding outwards is clearly visible. Author's collection

▼ A British Scout Carrier abandoned near Dunkerque (France) in Spring 1940. This tracked vehicle may have been captured and employed by a Wehrmacht unit as it shows German recognition signs. Private collection

THE UNIVERSAL CARRIER MK I

The proliferation of versions of a single machine to carry out a variety of roles was clearly a wasteful choice. Consequently in 1940, a Universal type of Carrier was introduced. The general construction of this armoured vehicle differed from the Bren Carrier.

The front remained basically unchanged but the protection of the rear compartments was now improved by full-length armour plates on both sides and at the rear.

The engine was still located centrally but its cover was modified. Four models, almost identical, of the Universal Carrier MK I existed. Since all of them employed the same power source, a Ford V8, the chief distinction was founded on the exact type of engine adopted. The British 79E 6004 CS or DS (65 hp) was identified by the number 1, the American EGAE 6004 US (85 hp) by the number 2, the American EGAEA 6004 US (85 hp) by the number 2A and the Canadian Co1UC 6097 ANH (95 hp) by the number 3. Therefore, a Universal Carrier No 2 MK I was a tracked vehicle produced in England and fitted with a EGAE 6004 US engine. Aveling-Barford, Ford, Nuffield, Sentinel Wagon, Thornycroft and Wolseley were all manufacturers of the MK I in England.

Carriers produced in Canada were designated as MK I* Universals (the asterisk indicates Canadian production). Generally, the main weapon installed in the gunner's compartment was either a .303 cal. Bren light machine gun or a .55 cal. Boys anti-tank rifle. Although all MK Is were provided with an aerial mounting bracket, only commanders' vehicles carried a radio (Wireless No 11 or No 19 set) as a rule.

The Universal Carrier had a payload of 13 cwt but this limit was often exceeded. When nothing else was available these vehicles were employed as artillery tractors for the British 6 pdr anti-tank gun, a role that had to be fulfilled only in emergency. The MK I was the base vehicle from which the further variants of the Universal Carrier were developed.

▲ Shown here is ANTELOPE, a British Universal Carrier MK I armed with a Bren light machine gun as well as a 2 inch mortar. This latter weapon, highly appreciated for its ability to deploy smoke, was fired from the engine cover plate of the vehicle. Author's collection

▼ Two German Pzkpfw IVs pass by a disabled Universal Carrier in 'Caunter' scheme. This is the same camouflage applied to two Bren Carriers shown on pages 13 and 14. It normally consisted of a tricolour disruptive design of Light Stone No 61 (a yellow sand) or Portland Stone No 64 (a pale cream) basic with Silver Grey No 28 (a medium yellow-green) and Slate No 34 (a dark grey-green) or Khaki Green G3 (close to olive drab) in angular stripes. North Africa, exact date unknown. Author's collection

▲ Indian troops in their MK Is not far from Keren (Eritrea). From 2 February to 27 March 1941, the rocky highlands near Keren witnessed a tough battle between Italian and British forces. Private collection

▼ In 1941, Great Britain supplied Greece with trucks, ambulances and armoured vehicles. Around 100 Universal Carrier MK Is were delivered to the Hellenic Army. The majority of them were destroyed or captured by the Germans. The light coloured hexagon painted on the right side of the vehicle is the marking of the 19th Greek Motorized Division. Note the aerial mast and its mounting. Private collection

▲ A Universal Carrier MK I fitted with an experimental armoured roof is followed by two Scout Carrier MK Is. Great Britain, 1941. Author's collection

▼Free French troops aboard a Universal Carrier in North Africa. Author's collection

▲ A Universal Carrier MK I photographed in Singapore. The vehicle is armed with two Bren light machine guns and a Boys anti-tank rifle. Note the 'Lucas style' British headlamps. US NARA

▼ A MK I of the Malta Garrison tows a trolley-load of 250-lb GP bombs. This Carrier is in Light Stone 61 or Portland Stone No 64 with a distinctive design of darker lines either in Khaki Green No 3 or in a dark brown hue. The resulting pattern resembled the rubble walls which bordered each and every Maltese field. Malta, November 1941. Private collection

▲ The left side of this Universal Carrier with full sand-shields is literally covered with Scottish phrases. North Africa, 27 October 1942. Private collection

▼ This Australian Carrier ran afoul of a minefield. Note the armoured wireless battery box with its open lid. Milne Bay (Papua New Guinea), 28 August 1942. Australian War Memorial

▲ A British MK I in Tunisia. A kit locker, of the type usually carried in the left-hand rear compartment, is fixed at the front. Private collection

▼ MK Is of 6th British Armoured Division move forward in Tunisia. Australian War Memorial

▲ Carriers were sometimes used to evacuate wounded soldiers. This picture shows stretcher-bearers of the 6th South African Armoured Division in training. Unknown location, Middle East, 2 September 1943. Private collection

▼ A column of Soviet Carriers sporting whitewash camouflage. The Red Army received different types of Carriers, including the American T16 which will be discussed further. US NARA

▲ Two MK Is of the 3rd County of London Yeomanry (Sharpshooters), 4th British Armoured Brigade, waiting at Catania port in Sicily prior to embarking for the Italian mainland. Sicily, September 1943. Private collection

▼ Carriers of the 3rd County of London Yeomanry arriving at Serracapriola (Province of Foggia, Italy). This armoured unit entered the town on October 1, 1943. A 4 inch smoke discharger is visible on the right side armour of the tracked vehicle in the foreground. Private collection

▲ A Scout Carrier (in the foreground) and a Universal Carrier MK I taking part in a demonstration in Perth (Australia), on March 27, 1943. The Scout Carrier is equipped with the typical Australian ribbed spoked bogie wheels. Australian War Memorial

▼ A Carrier of the 2nd New Zealand Division pictured in San Casciano (near Florence) on July 28, 1944. This tracked vehicle has a 7.92mm BESA installed at the rear, a machine gun extensively used by the British as a mounted weapon for armoured vehicle during the Second World War. A heavier, water-cooled Vickers is positioned in the gunner's compartment. A. Turnbull Library

▲ A Universal Carrier MK I named after the Indian town of KANGRA moves between Lanciano and Orsogna (Province of Chieti, Italy), on December 13, 1943. A German MG 42 is seen in the front weapon slot and a Bren with drum magazine is used in anti-aircraft role. This is a vehicle from the 6th Battalion, 13th Frontier Force Rifles, 19th Brigade, 8th Indian Infantry Division. Private collection

▲ East African troops of the British Army investigating a Universal Carrier MK I* recaptured from the Japanese. Burma, 1944. Private collection

▲ A MK I moving through the streets of Zagreb (Croatia) on May 7, 1945. Note the expedient armor on top of the driver's position and the additional machine guns mounted on the vehicle which probably came from a crashed German plane. This Carrier served with the People's Liberation Army of Yugoslavia. Private collection

▼Three 2nd New Zealand Division Carriers converted into ambulances. Sesto Imolese (Imola, Italy), April 1945. A. Turnbull Library

▲ Rear view of a New Zealand Ambulance Carrier based on the MK I variant. The rear plate was removed so that stretchers could be quickly loaded. The side plates have been extended to offer more protection. Faenza (Province of Ravenna, Italy), January 1945. A. Turnbull Library

▼ From late 1944, the Italian co-belligerent Army was entirely equipped with British, Canadian and American military vehicles. This picture shows a Universal Carrier of the 2nd Battalion, 21st Infantry Regiment, Italian Cremona Combat Group. Venice, late April 1945. Author's collection

▲ A Jewish Brigade Carrier with typical Canadian design headlights. The Jewish Brigade joined the British 8th Army in November 1944 and fought in the latter stages of the Italian campaign. Private collection

▼ The crew of a MK I* serving with a Canadian unit is greeted by civilians. Haarlem (Holland), 7 May 1945. Library Archives Canada

THE UNIVERSAL CARRIER MK II

First produced in early 1942, the Universal Carrier MK II was based on the MK I but embodied various modifications and was characterized by a new stowage arrangement.

The engine deck included a rack for two rifles and backrests for a Bren tripod and a Boys anti-tank rifle. A single masked headlamp was fitted to the left side of the gunner's compartment and two marker lights, one fixed to the water can holder, the other placed on the left front plate, were added. A small hinged flap was mounted above the frontal weapon slot while the angular folding flap on the gunner's compartment side armour to assist the driver view was deleted. A spare road wheel and a tow rope were carried at the front.

A new type of mudguard enclosed the front quarter of the top track run and two or four foot-steps were provided. Steel pipes were welded to the upper edge of the rear compartments armour, replacing all of the MK I rubber or timber firing rests. MK IIs also had a 2 inch mortar or a 4 inch smoke discharger, located on the inner left side of the gunner's compartment. A large kit locker was fixed across the rear of the upper hull.

As in the case of MK Is, MK IIs were sometimes fitted with simple towing hooks. In May 1944, the 'Stacey towing attachment' was introduced. This item was a sprung hook placed between two solid arms for emergency towing of the 6 pdr anti-tank gun. The MK II retained the same Ford V8 engine of the MK I. MK IIs produced in Great Britain were generally equipped with British or American engines.

Canadian built MK II*s were to have domestically-produced engines but the 95 hp unit was still under test by late 1943 and as a consequence large numbers of Carriers were fitted with 85 hp engines. Many existing MK I*s were also upgraded to the MK II* specification.

The term 'Welsh Guards Stowage' initially denoted a special configuration, intended for service in North Africa. It was a MK II* Carrier which had to be produced with a welded hull, new full-length sand-shields and a canvas cover. This type, with riveted hull and classic-style mudguards but without the cover, would affect the usual stowage pattern for the MK II Universal Carrier.

▲ A factory-fresh Universal Carrier MK II. This vehicle was built by Aveling-Barford. Maximum armour thickness of MK II was 3/8 inch (around 10 mm), the same as MK I. The steel pipe railing, originally developed to strengthen the longer side plates of the Windsor Carrier, was also adopted for Universal Carriers since the Summer of 1943. Private collection

▼ This MK II from the 59th British Infantry Division (Staffordshire) has been fully equipped for deep wading. The screens surrounding the upper hull are held in place by rods fixed to little brackets welded to the armour. Joints and openings of the riveted hull were treated with sealing materials. Author's collection

▲ A MK I* upgraded to MK II* specification. Note the 4 inch smoke discharger and the single lamp, still mounted on its original MK I bracket. Short sections of pipes are welded to the sides to hold foliage or other sorts of camouflage. The MK I mudguards were not usually replaced during upgrades. This Carrier belonged to the Lake Superior Regiment, the Motor Battalion of the 4th Armoured Brigade, 4th Canadian Armoured Division. Cintheaux (France), 8 August 1944. Library Archives Canada

▼ A Carrier from the Queen's Cameron Highlanders of Canada, 2nd Canadian Infantry Division waiting to move from Germany to Holland. This is another upgraded vehicle as revealed by the presence of the angular hinged flap on the gunner's compartment left side. Brackets for deep wading screens are welded to the hull. Leer (Germany), July 1945. Library Archives Canada

▲ A Universal Carrier MK II leads a column of vehicles from the 1st Polish Armoured Division. Scarborough (England) 17 July 1944. Narodowe Archiwum Cyfrowe

▼ The crew of this Universal Carrier MK II from the 1st Rifle Battalion, 3rd Rifle Brigade, 1st Polish Armoured Division, is pictured during a lull. England, July 1944. Narodowe Archiwum Cyfrowe

▲ A MK II* being loaded aboard a barge en route from South Beveland to North Beveland. It's a vehicle from the 8th Reconnaissance Regiment (14th Canadian Hussars), 2nd Canadian Infantry Division. Holland, 1 November 1944. Library Archives Canada

▲ A MK II of the 53rd British Infantry Division (Welsh) brings in a batch of prisoners. Welsh Division's 158th Brigade was tasked to cross the Escaut Canal near Lommel (Belgium) in order to continue the advance into Holland. The attack, conducted between 17 and 18 September 1944, met fierce resistance from German paratroopers. Private collection

▼ A British Universal Carrier MK II rolling in Aalst (Holland) with a 6 pdr anti-tank gun in tow on September 18, 1944. This vehicle, fitted with the 'Stacey towing attachment', served with the Guards Armoured Division. Nationaal Archief

▲ The crew of a MK II Universal Carrier from 8th Battalion Rifle Brigade, 11th Armoured Division, hands out chocolate to Dutch youngsters. Holland, 22 September 1944. Private collection

▲ A MK II of 11th Royal Scots Fusiliers, 49th British Infantry Division (West Riding). Note the divisional sign, a polar bear standing on a ice floe, reminiscent of the service in Iceland between 1940 and 1942. The white 61 on a green square identified the 2nd Battalion of the 2nd Brigade in an infantry division. The vehicle illustrated was probably built by Sentinel Wagon. Author's collection

▼ Luxembourgers of the 1st Belgian Brigade inside their MK II* during a parade. The use of thin metal strips bent over the upper edge of the rear compartments armour was a typical feature of Canadian produced MK II*s. The Canadian-style marker light positioned near the main headlamp is of interest. Luxembourg, 28 July 1945. Private collection

▲ The No 2 MK II* designation is also referred to the 'Welsh Guards Stowage' configuration, initially required for British orders. Private collection

▼ After the end of German occupation, the fragile pro-Allies Greek government rapidly disintegrated. As a result, in December 1944 an uprising broke out in Athens. British forces sided for the right-wing organizations against the communists. This photo, taken in the Greek Capital, shows two MK Is upgraded to MK II specification (on the right) and what appears to be a 'Welsh Guards Stowage' MK II* with full-length sand-shields (on the left). Private collection

THE UNIVERSAL CARRIER MK III

The MK III was the last Mark of the Universal Carrier range. Its external appearance was strikingly similar to that of the MK II with which it is often confused. A closer look at the vehicle reveals that unlike the MK I and the MK II which both had a riveted hull, the MK III was of welded construction. The floor was reinforced, in order to provide better protection against mine damage. The thicknesses of the lower rear armour and of the front mudguards were also increased. Another major aspect to consider was the division plate that separated the front and rear compartments: looking carefully at the available pictures one can see that the air intake above the front seats was deleted. Compared to its predecessors, the engine cover of the MK III was different, having additional grilles on a new stepped deck. Ford of Canada was the main manufacturer of these Carriers, designated as MK III* Universals. It seems that the only batch of British MK IIIs (T 331701 – T 334900) was built by Ford of Britain at Dagenham (London).

▼ A Universal Carrier MK III* of the 49th Reconnaissance Regiment, 49th British Infantry Division (West Riding). Holland, Spring 1945. Private collection

▲ The MK III* came into service in late 1943. The hull is of welded construction: the armour plates weren't assembled with riveted joints. Here, a MK III* of an unidentified unit races through the ruins of Masendorf (Germany), 17 April 1945. Private collection

▼ This MK III* served with the Motor Battalion of the 1st Czechoslovak Independent Armoured Brigade which landed in Normandy during the summer of 1944. On arrival the Brigade moved to Falaise where it became part of the Canadian 1st Army. It was then given the task to besiege the German-held port of Dunkirk until the end of the war. Library Archives Canada

▲ A MK III* of the 1st Belgian Infantry Brigade, also known as 'Brigade Piron' after its commander, Jean-Baptiste Piron. This vehicle carries a white 'B', the original formation sign. A small Belgian roundel is superimposed on the Allied white star on the upper hull side. The 'Brigade Piron', consisting of Belgian and Luxembourgish soldiers, took part in the liberation of Belgium. Private collection

▲ A MK III* from the Princess Irene Brigade, a unit composed of Dutch soldiers arrived in Great Britain after the German invasion of Holland. The formation sign, an heraldic lion rampant of the House of Orange-Nassau (in orange on a black disc) and the title 'IRENE' (in white), are seen on this Carrier. The number 112 in white on a red square identifies the 3rd Motorized Fighting Group of the Brigade. Holland, May 1945. Nationaal Archief

▼ The 1st British Airborne Division used a small number of modified MK III* Universals during Operation 'Market Garden'. The modifications, mainly intended to reduce weight and size, included the addition of brackets for carrying a 3 inch mortar on the rear plate, a particular barely visible in this poor but unique photo. US NARA

▲ The crew of this Mk III* serving with the 4th Battalion (Wiltshire Regiment), 43rd British Infantry Division (Wessex), takes a rest. The absence of the air intake on the divisional plate is noteworthy. The headlamp and the rearview mirror have been relocated on this Carrier. Holland, 21 September 1944. Private collection

THE ARMOURED OBSERVATION POST CARRIER (AOP MK I, MK II, MK III)

The Armoured Observation Post (AOP) Carriers were produced for the Royal Artillery. The AOP MK I, based on the Scout Carrier, had a cable reel fitted on the rear, mounted at the right-hand side of the battery box. A special vision port designed to accommodate binoculars for the Artillery Forward Observation Officer was incorporated in the left frontal armour. The left-hand side of the engine cover was modified and the top received an extra grille. The AOP No 1 MK II was essentially a Universal Carrier MK I with AOP fittings, carrying No 11 and No 18 (man-portable) Wireless Sets, signal flares and signalling lamps. On these vehicles, the cable reel was placed on the left-hand rear mudguard. The welded hull AOP No 1 MK III, produced solely by Ford of Britain, had an additional cable reel at the front. This variant, equipped with either the No 11 or the No 19 Wireless Set, sported a single headlamp centrally mounted at the front and two marker lights. A ladder rack was fixed to the left side of the upper hull.

▼ A 2nd New Zealand Division AOP MK II pictured in North Africa. The white X indicated the commander's vehicle of a battery of a Field Artillery Regiment. The New Zealand national emblem, a white fern leaf on a black square, was the unit sign adopted by the division. AOP MK IIs were built by Aveling-Barford and Sentinel Wagon. A. Turnbull Library

▲ Rear view of one of the 253 AOP MK IIs built by Aveling-Barford between September 1939 and March 1940. Note the larger battery box with attached petrol and oil can holder. The cable reel is located on the left mudguard. The vehicle carries the badge of the 52nd British Infantry Division (Lowland), a white St. Andrew's cross on blue shield. England, 1 November 1941. Private collection

▲ Another view of the AOP MK II of the previous photo. The holder for the Artillery Board No 3 is fitted on the hull side. The artillery board could be used for the graphic solution of problems involving map references, targets coordinates and ranges. The white 42 on a red over blue background indicated the senior Field Artillery Regiment of an Infantry Division while the white X on a blue square with red lower left quadrant identified the commander's vehicle of the 3rd Battery. Private collection

▼ An AOP MK III from the 1st Polish Motorized Artillery Regiment, 1st Polish Armoured Division, photographed in a British town. Although the white 76 on a red over blue square which denoted a Field Artillery Regiment of an Armoured Division is present, the vehicle still carries the emblem of the 1st Polish Corps on the left mudguard. Narodowe Archiwum Cyfrowe

▲ This AOP MK III from the 15th British Infantry Division (Scottish), moves on the bridge over the Odon river in Tourme-auville (Normandy) during the final phases of Operation Epsom (late June 1944). Author's collection

THE 3 IN MORTAR CARRIER (MK I AND MK II)

The '3 inch mortar', whose precise caliber was 3.209 inch despite the official designation, entered British service in the 1930s. Initially the mortar was carried into position by its crew or by a truck, but as the war progressed the Army made common use of a Carrier in transporting the disassembled weapon with its ammunition. The production of the 3 in Mortar Carrier started in late 1940, when Wolseley began building the first batch of 400 No 1 MK Is with modified stowage arrangement to accommodate the mortar tube, bipod and base plate at the rear. Factory built MK I Mortar Carriers usually lacked firing rests on the upper edge of rear compartments vertical plates. A number of MK I* Universal Carriers were converted into the mortar role using kits produced in England. The MK II Mortar Carrier (No 1 and No 2) was first produced by Sentinel Wagon in early 1942. Mortar Carrier designations didn't strictly coincide with those of the Universal Carrier. In many cases, earlier vehicles were classified as MK IIs even if they were based on MK I hulls. Obviously, it is correct to say that Mortar Carriers which used later Universal hulls with squared valances and single headlamp, were certainly designated as MK IIs. The 3 inch mortar was generally dismounted to fire but photographic evidence shows that the weapon was occasionally operated from inside the vehicle. Some selected Mortar Carriers were equipped with a No 18 Wireless Set.

▼ A Ford of Canada built Mortar Carrier towing a 6 pdr anti-tank gun. The 1944 modification to accommodate the base plate on the glacis is almost completely obscured by the spare road wheels of the gun carriage and tracked vehicle. This Carrier served with the 3rd Anti-tank Regiment, 3rd Canadian Infantry Division, in northwestern Europe. Library Archives Canada.

▲ Thornycroft converted a MK I Universal (census number T 12844) into the first prototype Mortar Carrier. Ammunition tubes were carried inside the vehicle: 54 held in frames located into both rear compartments (30 on the left and 24 on the right) and 12 stored at the front (6 on either side). The vehicle is still fitted with firing rests above the rear compartments armour plates. Private collection

▲ Rear view of the Thornycroft's prototype with the stowage arrangement adopted for the majority of Mortar Carriers. The battery box was deleted to permit the mounting of the mortar tube, secured to special brackets above its cleaning rod and below the starting handle. The MK I can holder was relocated to the left side, the base plate was stowed on the right. The bipod was carried on the rear deck. Private collection

▲ An Italian paratrooper of the Folgore Division poses near a captured Mortar Carrier in North Africa. Private collection

▼ EDNA, a 3 in Mortar Carrier from the Dutch Princess Irene Brigade, is seen here during the victory parade held in Amsterdam on May 31, 1945. It is built on a MK I hull whose gunner's compartment lacked the hinged angular folding flap on the side armour. Nationaal Archief

▲ Attempts were made to use the 3 inch mortar from the gunner's compartment as demonstrated by this picture, showing a Carrier from the 1/6th Battalion, Queen's Royal Regiment, 131st Brigade, 7th British Armoured Division. Scafati (Province of Salerno, Italy), September 1943. Author's collection

▼ Another shot of a 3 inch mortar being fired from inside a Carrier, in this case a vehicle of the 2nd British Infantry Division. Burma, 1945. Private collection

▲ A Mortar Carrier MK II (in the foreground) and a Medium Machine Gun Carrier of the Irish Guards Group, Guards Armoured Division, photographed in Aalst (Holland) on 18 September 1944. The Mortar Carrier mounts Loyd Carrier wheels with circular lightening holes. Wikimedia

▼ A disabled MK II Mortar Carrier fitted with brackets for securing deep wading panels. Mortar Carriers based on MK II hulls were built without the metal tubing on the upper edge of the rear compartments vertical plates. Northwestern Europe, 1944. Private collection

▲ Mortar Carriers of the 2nd Battalion, Essex Regiment, 56th Brigade, 49th British Infantry Division (West Riding). The nearest vehicle (census number T 226376) is a Wolseley built MK II Mortar Carrier. Holland, 13 April 1945. Library Archives Canada

▼ A Mortar Carrier MK II of the Goito Bersaglieri Battalion, Special Infantry Regiment, Legnano Italian Combat Group, moving in liberated Bologna (Italy) on 21 April 1945. Two C 224 ammunition boxes are fixed to the glacis. Author's collection

▲ Alpini (Italian mountain troops) from the 2nd Battalion, Special Infantry Regiment, Legnano Italian Combat Group, aboard their Wolseley built Mortar Carrier MK II. Note the typical position of the marker lights mounted on the front armour plate and the writing MILANO on right front mudguard. Bologna (Italy), 21 April 1945. Author's collection

THE MEDIUM MACHINE GUN CARRIER (MMG MK I AND MK II)

In order to increase the firepower of the infantry, a number of MK I and MK II Universal Carriers were armed with a water-cooled, .303 cal. Vickers medium machine gun in early 1943. The weapon, ideal for supporting offensive operations, was mounted on the vehicle's engine deck and could be fired in any direction. Medium Machine Gun (MMG) Carriers were above all grouped in Machine Gun Battalions of British infantry divisions and Independent Machine Gun Companies of British armoured divisions. The MMG Carrier equipment, which always included the machine gun tripod, ammunitions boxes and a smoke-discharger, varied. For example, the platoon's commander MMG MK II was also fitted with a Wireless Set No 22 and had a signal pistol, a case for maps and a megaphone (like the one found in Mortar Carriers) whilst other Carriers like those used by platoon sergeants carried a PIAT (Projectory Infantry Anti-Tank) grenade-launcher with its ammunition besides the machine gun. There is evidence of field modified Universal Carriers equipped with other types of machine guns.

▼ A Canadian Medium Machine Gun MK I* Carrier. Italy, 1944. Library Archives Canada

▲ When the engine deck mounting for the Vickers wasn't available, the weapon could be installed in the gunner's compartment as in the case of this MK I* from the 2/7th Battalion, Middlesex Regiment, photographed in Italy in 1944. The red/white/red rectangle shown on the hull side and repeated on the front was a recognition marking officially adopted in early 1942, used on some British armoured vehicles in the Italian war theater before the introduction of the white Allied star. Wikimedia

▼ AMI and ADA, two MMG Carriers (based on MK I hulls) of the Saskatoon Light Infantry, 5th Canadian Infantry Division, pictured near Monacilioni (Province of Campobasso, Italy), October 1943. Library Archives Canada

▲ A Medium Machine Gun MK II Carrier of the 1st Independent Motorized Fighting Group, Princess Irene Brigade. Stowage fittings for a shovel and a pick axe, additional tools to be used for digging-in the British Vickers machine gun, are visible on the glacis. National Archief

▼ Three MMG MK IIs from the 2nd Independent Machine Gun Company, 11th British Armoured Division. Sentinel Wagon and Thornycroft were the main manufacturers of the MMG Carrier. Germany, spring 1945. Author's collection

▲ The Toronto Scottish Regiment fought as part of the 2nd Canadian Infantry Division in northwestern Europe until the end of the war. This MMG MK II shows the Independent Machine Gun Battalion tactical sign, a white 64 on black background. The lifting jack is stowed on the right front mudguard. Nieuport (Belgium), 9 September 1944. Library Archives Canada

▲ This 2nd New Zealand Division MK I Carrier was pressed into service heavily armed: besides a British .303 cal. Bren light machine gun, it also mounted two American well-known weapons, a .30 cal. M1919 Browning medium machine gun and a .50 cal. M2 Browning heavy machine gun. Borgo San Giuliano, Rimini (Italy), 22 September 1944. A. Turnbull Library

▼ Although welded hull MK IIIs weren't converted into MMG Carriers, they were sometimes fitted with other weapons. The MK III seen here is armed with a .50 cal Browning heavy machine gun. Northwestern Europe, 26 April 1945. Private collection

THE LOYD CARRIER (TPC, TT, TCL AND TS&C)

In 1938, Vivian G. Loyd, who had previously worked with John V. Carden on the development of British tankettes, left Vickers-Armstrong and founded a new company. In that same period, he presented a prototype of a low-cost tracked vehicle that would lead to the Loyd Carrier, a multifunction machine based upon the reversed chassis of a British Fordson 4x2 15 cwt truck, fitted with a couple of Horstmann suspension two-wheel bogies on each side. The driver sat centrally at the front of an open-topped hull and steering was assisted by sprockets mounted both front and rear. Two marks of the Loyd Carrier existed. The difference laid in the type of brakes adopted for the vehicle. The MK I was equipped with a brake system produced by the American corporation Bendix, the MK II had a British brake system, produced by Girling and introduced at a later date. As with the Universal Carrier, the Loyd Carrier was also classified according to the origin of the Ford V8 engine fitted. The protection of the mild steel body could benefit from 7 mm of maximum armour if the so-called 'BP plates' were bolted to the front and sides. After successful tests conducted in 1939, the British War Office placed an order for 200 Loyd Carriers. These initial vehicles, all produced by Vivian Loyd & Co., were of the Tracked, Personnel Carrying type (TPC), primarily intended to transport troops or supplies. The production soon moved to other firms like Arnfield, Aveling-Barford, Dennis, Ford, Harland Engineering, MB Wild, Sentinel Wagon and Wolseley, making possible the appearance of additional variants, including the well-known Carrier, Tracked Towing (TT), widely used to tow a 6 pdr anti-tank gun or a 10 cwt trailer containing a 4.2 inch mortar and to transport related ammunition. The Loyd TT was originally developed for the 2 pdr anti-tank gun but it seems that the carriage was prone to damage if towed over rough terrain, so wheeled vehicles like trucks were later required for transporting these artillery pieces loaded on cargo beds. The Carrier, Tracked, Cable Layer (TCL), designed for the Royal Signal Corps units, transported spools of telegraph wire, ladders and poles. In order to provide electrical assistance to armoured vehicles, over 2,000 Loyd Carriers were equipped with 30V and 12V generators for engine starting and battery charging. The list of carried items included heavy tank batteries, a hydrometer, a voltmeter, jars for distilled water, starter cables. Designated Carrier, Tracked, Starting & Charging (TS&C), they were mainly issued to armoured regiments.

▲ A Loyd Carrier towing a 6 pdr anti-tank gun. Two side shields, which offered more protection to the weapon and crew, are carried on the vehicle's sides. Holland, September 1944. Nationaal Archief

▼ A Canadian Loyd TPC (Tracked, Personnel Carrying) armed with a Vickers medium machine gun. Note the exposed front axle. The engine is placed at the rear of the vehicle. Library Archives Canada

▲ Left side view of a Loyd Carrier. The canopy was a standard item. Author's collection

▼ Some 15,000 Loyd TT (Tracked, Towing) were produced. This one was photographed in London in 1944. Wikimedia

▲ Left front three quarter view of a Loyd TCL (Tracked, Cable Layer). The cable layer mechanism was fitted behind the driver's position. Private collection

▼ A Loyd Carrier returns to a British beach after the unfortunate Dieppe raid of August 19, 1942. US NARA

▲ A Loyd Carrier TT serving with 53rd British Infantry Division (Welsh) moves along a railway line in the vicinity of 's-Hertogenbosch. This vehicle mounts wheels with circular lightening holes. Holland, 25 October 1944. Wikimedia

▼ This Polish Loyd Carrier was photographed in Italy. A stowage box was often carried above the front axle of these tracked vehicles. Narodowe Archiwum Cyfrowe

▲ A Loyd TT towing a 10 cwt trailer, used for transporting the 4.2 inch mortar. This Carrier served with 1/8th Middlesex Regiment, the machine gun battalion of the 43rd British Infantry Division (Wessex). The unit sign, a yellow wyvern on a blue square, expressed the link between the division and the ancient traditions of the Anglo-Saxon Kingdom of Wessex. Odon Valley, west of Caen (Normandy), 16 July 1944. Wikimedia

▼ A Loyd Carrier from the Italian co-belligerent Friuli Combat Group advances towards Bologna with a 6 pdr anti-tank gun in tow. The end of the war in Italy is near. Author's collection

THE T16 (MK I AND MK II)

It was soon clear that Universal Carriers suffered serious problems under heavy loads. The main concerns were related to suspension and drive train failures. Important experimental works aimed at the improvement of these tracked vehicles were carried out in the United States and resulted in an almost completely new machine, designated T16 MK I. The production, exclusively intended for Britain and Commonwealth armies, started at Ford's Somerville plant near Boston (Massachusetts). Like the Loyd Carrier, the T16 had a brake-steering mechanism. A higher, sloping glacis plate was designed to allow for the four tiller bar levers with which the vehicle was steered: the outer two were used for gradual turns, the inner for major changes in direction. The longer open-topped welded hull rested on two-wheel units, two each side. The Ford V8 engine was centrally mounted as per other Carriers but sported twin exhaust pipes over the rear armour plate. During the war, T16 MK Is were used as 6 pdr anti-tank gun tractors and 4.2 inch mortar carriers, mostly by Canadian forces. In order to improve stability and increase the vehicle's payload, a modified version of the T16 MK I with altered bogie spacing, known as MK II but officially designated as Universal Carrier T16 E2, was built by Ford of Britain in late 1945.

▲ A T16 MK I intended to act as a 6 pdr anti-tank gun tractor. Ammunition cases are stored in the rear compartments. The British census number (59234) is correctly preceded by the letter T, adopted to identify tanks and tracked carriers. The C prefix indicated that the vehicle was assigned to Canadian Army. Library Archives Canada

▲ A T16 MK I of the 3rd Canadian Infantry division towing a 6 pdr anti-tank gun. A closer look at the photo reveals the presence of the unit badge on the rear fender, a golden yellow maple leaf on a blue-grey rectangle. The T16 was about 11 inches longer than the Universal Carrier. Caen (Normandy), August 1944. US NARA

▼ The Canadian Army used the T 16 to transport the 4.2 inch mortar and its ammunition. The mortar tube and bipod were stowed on the engine cover while the base plate was attached to the gunner's compartment at the front. Generally, a special mortar base plate to be used on soft grounds was carried on the left side armour. Author's collection

▲ This T16 belonging to a Canadian Anti-Tank Regiment mounted wheels with different cast spokes. Ford's Somerville plant produced 13,893 T16 Carriers. Holland, 13 April 1945. Library Archives Canada

▼ Mortar Platoon commander's T16s carried cable reels for communication between crews. These Carriers were also equipped with both No 18 and No 19 wireless sets. Library Archives Canada

▲ Front view of a T16 serving with the 1st Battalion, The Black Watch (Royal Highland Regiment), 5th Brigade, 2nd Canadian Infantry division. South Beveland (Holland), 30 September 1944. Library Archives Canada

▲ A mortar section commander's T16 MK I. As with all British and Canadian vehicles, this Carrier sports a yellow disc bearing a digit in black paint, indicating its rough weight in tons (4 in this case). A vehicle could only cross a bridge marked with the same or greater numerical designation. Library Archives Canada

▼ A T16 from 1st Battalion, Cameron Highlanders of Ottawa, 3rd Canadian Infantry Division loaded onto a LVT (Landing Vehicle, Tracked). Whereas the Loyd Carrier steering was activated by a pair of levers, the T16 was somewhat more difficult to drive, since steering was accomplished through use of four tillers. Rees (vicinity), Germany, 24 March 1945. Library Archives Canada

THE WINDSOR CARRIER MK I*

The Windsor Carrier MK I* was an open-type tracked vehicle with riveted armour produced in 5,000 units by Ford of Canada from 1944 to 1945. Designed for transporting support weapons and towing anti-tank guns along with ammunition and crew members, it maintained the steering system of the earlier Carriers. Although the Windsor had a front section nearly identical to that of the MK II* Universal, it was longer. Like the T16, this Canadian Carrier mounted a couple of two-wheel bogie assemblies for better stability but with spring dampeners facing forward. Four roof bows and a tarp were provided for protection against bad weather. The Windsor Carrier was used in limited numbers during the final stages of the war in Europe.

▲ A Windsor MK I* serving with 1/5th Battalion, Queen's Royal Regiment, 131st Infantry Brigade, 7th British Armoured Division with a 6 pdr anti-tank gun in tow. This type of Carrier took its name from Windsor (Ontario), the southernmost Canadian city, in which Ford of Canada plants were located. The cleaning rod of the gun is carried on the left side of the vehicle. Germany, Spring 1945. Private collection

▲ Windsor Carriers from 9th Rifle Battalion, 3rd Infantry Brigade, 1st Polish Armoured Division. The Windsor (172 inches long) could be considered as an elongated version of the Universal Carrier MK II* (144 inches long). It was powered by a 95 hp engine. Narodowe Archiwum Cyfrowe

▼ Another photograph showing Windsor Carriers and 6 pdr anti-tank guns of the 1st Polish Armoured Division. The Windsor was employed in the same way as the T16. Narodowe Archiwum Cyfrowe

▲ A Windsor Carrier belonging to 49th Reconnaissance Regiment, 49th British Infantry Division (West Riding), advances in Amersfoort (Holland) on May 7, 1945. Folding brackets for the 6 pdr anti-tank gun extra shields are fitted on the right side of the vehicle. The 'Polar Bear Division' played a part in the liberation of Utrecht province. Nationaal Archief

▼ A picture of a Windsor MK I* from the 49th British Reconnaissance Regiment showing the typical rear hull locker. The Windsor was some 18 inch longer and 1 ton heavier than the T16. Unknown location, Utrecht province (Holland), 7 May 1945. Nationaal Archief

THE FLAMETHROWER UNIVERSAL CARRIERS

It was only with the fall of France in 1940 that the British began to consider the possibility of mounting flamethrowers on vehicles, including Universal Carriers. The first device to be produced was the Ronson, a pressure operated flamethrower developed by the Petroleum Warfare Department. Available by late 1942, it was nonetheless rejected by the British War Office. Further improvements led to the FT transportable No 2 MK I better known as the Wasp Mk I, first built in September 1943, characterized by a large flame projector and two fuel-flame tanks to be stowed within the rear compartments of a Universal Carrier. However, like the Ronsons, MK Is were soon relegated to training purposes, since in August 1943 the prototype of the FT transportable No 2 MK II, the so-called Wasp MK II, was successfully tested. Boasting a completely new flame projector, it was clearly superior to the MK I but its flame-fuel tanks (40 and 60 gallons) were, once again, placed inside the Carrier. The Canadian Army ordered the Wasp MK II kit but required it to have only a single 75-gallon flame-fuel tank, fitted outside at the rear. In this way, the vehicle kept the space to accommodate a third crew member in the right rear compartment and could therefore be used as a regular Universal Carrier without dismantling the flamethrower and its equipment. Flamethrower Carriers with this modification were designated Wasp MK IIC (the letter C stands for Canada). Conversions of the MK II into the MK IIC variant were made by mounting the 60-gallon flame-fuel tank at the rear.

▲ A MK I* Universal converted into a Ronson flamethrower Carrier mounting two external flame-fuel tanks. The flame projector is installed on the front gunner's compartment armour. Canadian Ronsons were only used for training purposes.

▲ A Wasp MK II with dual internal fuel tanks and improved flame projector mounted within the gunner's compartment. This variant was built between August 1943 and June 1944. Private collection

▲ Canadian made Wasps are recognizable by the large external fuel tank. The 2nd New Zealand Division received some MK IICs which were used during the final offensive in the Po Valley. This flamethrower Carrier, based on a MK I Universal, was photographed in Sesto Imolese (vicinity of Bologna, Italy) on April 16, 1945. A. Turnbull Library

▼ This picture shows a Wasp MK IIC from 4th Battalion, Wiltshire Regiment, 129th Brigade, 43rd British Infantry Division (Wessex), flaming the barracks of the Bergen-Belsen concentration camp, liberated on April 15, 1945. Lower Saxony (Germany), Spring 1945. Private collection

▲ A Wasp MK IIC serving with Les Fusiliers Mont-Royal, 6th Brigade, 2nd Canadian Infantry Division moves forward in Beilen (Drenthe Province, Holland) on April 12, 1945. A Canadian built eight-tube smoke discharger is fitted to the front. Nationaal Archief

▼ A Wasp MK IIC fitted with 'plastic armour', an additional protection applied on the front and side plates of driver and flamethrower operator's compartment. Library Archives Canada

▲ Crew members are filling up the flame-fuel tanks of their Wasps MK IIC. Both Carriers shown here are equipped with 'plastic armour', fitted inside and outside the front section. Author's collection

▼ Two Wasps MK IIC of 9th Rifle Battalion, 3rd Infantry Brigade, 1st Polish Armoured Division. The Flamethrower Carrier on the left is based on a Universal MK II, the one on the right on a Universal MK III . Narodowe Archiwum Cyfrowe

▲ Dutch civilians ride on a Wasp MK IIC of 7th Reconnaissance Regiment (17th Duke of York's Royal Canadian Hussars), 3rd Canadian Infantry Division. Zwolle (Holland), April 1945. Library Archives Canada

AUSTRALIAN AND NEW ZEALAND LOCAL PATTERN CARRIERS (LP1 AND LP2)

Both Australia and New Zealand produced their own types of Carrier, based on Bren No 2 MK Is imported from Great Britain. The first Australian design was an armoured vehicle of riveted construction, the Carrier, Machine Gun (Aust) LP1, introduced in 1940. Unlike its British counterpart it had a raised glacis, needed to accommodate the two tillers which actuated the brakes. This steering system proved to be a problem as it caused serious brake wear. The Australian LP1 was usually armed with a water-cooled Vickers machine gun mounted on a pintle located just under the enlarged firing slot in the gunner's compartment. Two storage lockers, one on top of the other, were attached on the right side of the hull. Approximately 160 LP1 Carriers were built by Victorian Railways at the Newport Workshops in Melbourne. Although the majority of these machines remained in Australia for training, some were transported overseas and operated by Australian Army in the Middle East (Syria, Palestine, Egypt). The New Zealand produced Bren No 2 MK I was on the contrary unarmoured, having a hull made from mild-steel plates. It used the same steering mechanism adopted for the British Bren Carrier, to which it strongly resembled. Subsequent Australian models, known as the Carrier, Machine Gun (Aust) LP2 and LP2A, looked more similar to the Universal Carrier. LP2 and LP2A were nearly identical and externally indistinguishable. The only difference is that LP2 was fitted with a Ford commercial truck 1938-type rear axle while LP2A came with a 1940-type rear axle. Both vehicles had a welded hull and incorporated a track warping and braking mechanism. The LP2 (first produced in 1941) and the LP2A were manufactured by Victorian Railways, South Australian Railways, Metropolitan Gas Company, Ford Motor Company and State Engineering Works. To overcome engine overheating, a large air intake was installed above the divisional plate. Five bins were mounted across the rear for the stowage of various equipment. During the war, these Carriers were mainly employed throughout Australia but a number were shipped to Malaya and New Guinea. An Australian LP2 was used as a template to produce New Zealand copies, designated Carrier, Machine Gun LP2 and LP2A (NZ), which were later slightly modified to carry a Bren in the gunner's compartment. A lengthened hull of an Australian LP2 provided the basis for the Carrier, Anti-tank 2 pdr (Aust), armed with a 2 pdr gun placed on a revolving platform at the rear. To allow this modification, the engine was shifted forward to the left of the driver's compartment. By the time this version came into service, it was already obsolete as the enemy vehicles had thicker armour that couldn't be penetrated by 2 pdr anti-tank rounds. Another variant of the LP2, called Carrier, 3in Mortar (Aust), also appeared. Developed around the Anti-tank Carrier, it transported a 3 inch mortar fitted on the rear deck planned for the 2 pdr gun.

▲ A Carrier, Machine Gun (Aust) LP1 manned by Australian troops. The front section shows a higher sloping glacis, needed to accommodate the steering levers. Australian War Memorial

▼ Right side view of a Carrier, Machine Gun (Aust) LP1. Note the riveted construction together with the twin storage lockers. Australian built machines were equipped with ribbed spoke bogie wheels. Darwin, Northern Territory (Australia), July 1940.

▲ A New Zealand Bren No 2 MK I. This tracked vehicle used the same steering system as the British Bren Carrier. Private collection

▼ The crew of a Carrier, Machine Gun (Aust) LP2 pay a call on the rear gunner of an American bomber before a raid over Japanese bases. New Guinea, 1942. Australian War Memorial

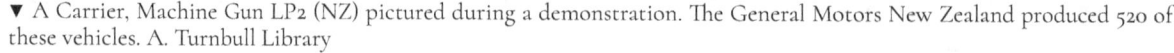

▲ Left side view of a Carrier, Machine Gun (Aust) LP2. This vehicle had the early design of stowage layout as tools are carried on the hull side. Australian War Memorial

▼ A Carrier, Machine Gun LP2 (NZ) pictured during a demonstration. The General Motors New Zealand produced 520 of these vehicles. A. Turnbull Library

▲ An Australian Anti-tank 2 pdr Carrier of later design with two air scoops on the glacis plate. These Carriers were only used for training. Australian War Memorial

▼ A closer view of the Carrier, Anti-tank 2 pdr (Aust). The artillery piece is fitted on a turntable. Australian War Memorial

▲ The Carrier, 3in Mortar (Aust). Even if the mortar could be operated directly from the vehicle's platform, a conventional base plate, to be used for firing the weapon on the ground, was carried on the left side of the vehicle. Mortar bombs were stored along the rear compartment sides. Note the bins for stowing equipment at the rear. Australian War Memorial

▼ Three-quarter rear view of the Carrier, 3in Mortar (Aust). All the 400 Mortar Carriers produced in Australia were sent abroad as aid during the final stages of the war. Australian War Memorial

PROTOTYPES, SPECIALIZED VARIANTS AND FIELD MODIFICATIONS

We conclude this book with a quick review of the most important Carrier prototypes, variants and field modifications. Some of these vehicles saw service, others were never used operationally. The list, almost endless, includes Carriers designed for a variety of roles, fitted with artillery pieces, turrets, plows, bridge sections, carpet-layer mechanisms, floatation mattresses and mine exploders. Many efforts were directed to the conversion of regular Carriers into self-propelled guns. For example, the VA D50 chassis was soon adapted to mount a Vickers 40 mm gun.

The Carrier, Anti-tank, 2 pdr was, on the contrary, a newly built vehicle of the same type, consisting of an unarmoured Machine Gun Carrier armed with a 2 pdr anti-tank gun placed behind a fixed shield. For their part, the Canadians produced about 100 MK I* Universals equipped with a 2 pdr anti-tank gun fitted on the engine cover and protected by a slightly altered 6 pdr anti-tank gun inner shield. These light tank hunters were only used by Canadian Army for training as their weapons rapidly became ineffective against the thicker plates of newly developed enemy armoured vehicles.

A number of self-propelled anti-aircraft and anti-tank guns were also based on the Loyd Carrier but none passed the prototype stage. The Germans captured numerous Carriers which were nonetheless used as self-propelled guns during the war.

One of the most spectacular derivatives of the Carrier was the Praying Mantis. The final version of this British vehicle was based upon a MK I Universal chassis mounting a pivoting armoured body for a two-man crew, completed with a small turret containing a pair of Bren light machine guns. When the body was elevated, the Carrier was able to fire over obstacles like walls, trees and hedgerows, without exposing most of its silhouette, thus revealing the reason for the name adopted, borrowed from the well-known predatory insect.

Trials showed that the Praying Mantis was a complicated vehicle and as a consequence the project was abandoned in 1944. The Conger MK I was a British concussion type mine exploder carried on a towed Universal Carrier. The engine and other vehicle components were removed to get the necessary space for the special equipment, made up of a tank full of nitroglycerin (822c) and a projector. This device launched a five inch rocket trailing an empty hose (330 feet long) which, once deployed on a minefield, was filled with 2,500 pounds of liquid explosive. The detonation of the nitroglycerin could clear a 20 feet wide lane.

Used by the 79th British Armoured Division near Calais in September 1944, the Conger was later abandoned as it was found to be a dangerous weapon for its operators. Despite not being part of the Carrier family in the strict sense, the Canadian Armoured Snowmobile MK I, produced in 1944, is the last machine which deserves to be mentioned here, just because it was equipped with the same axle mounted on the American T16.

▲ The VA D50 mounting a Vickers 40 mm anti-tank gun. It was never used operationally. Private collection

▼ The Carrier, Anti-tank, 2 pdr was based on the Machine Gun Carrier. Note the ammunition racks on the right side of the fighting compartment. This vehicle retained the early large armoured headlamps at the front. Private collection

▲ A Universal Carrier MK I, armed with a Hotchkiss 25 mm Anti-tank gun model 1934, used by Free French troops in North Africa. Private collection

▼ The Canadian Tank Hunter, equipped with a 2 pdr Anti-tank gun mounted on a modified and strengthened engine cover of a MK I* Universal Carrier. Ammunition holders were fitted along the sides and the division plate at the rear. Library Archives Canada

▲ A Universal Carrier MK I in German service, armed with a 2,8 cm sPzb.41 (schwere Panzerbüchse 41) anti-tank gun. This vehicle retained its original caunter camouflage scheme. Vicinity of Benghazi (Lybia), 1942. Private collection

▼ A captured MK I Universal equipped with three Panzerschrecks and four Panzerfausts, serving with the 3rd Panzergrenadier Division. This kind of vehicles were designated by the Germans as 8,8 cm Panzerschreck-Raketen auf Bren Carrier (e). Italy, early 1944. Bundesarchiv

▲ Various Carriers, captured in the Western Desert, inspired two Italian projects, the CVP-5, based on the L6/40 Light Tank and the CVP-4 seen here, armed with a 8 mm Breda machine gun and provided with two-wheel suspension bogies which were copies of those used on British Universals. Both vehicles had never seen service. Private collection

▼ New Zealand engineers testing a Universal Carrier MK I equipped with an experimental floatation device. Maadi, Nile River (Egypt), August 1943. A. Turnbull Library

▲ Two rows of seven PIAT grenade launchers were mounted by the Canadians at the rear of some Universal Carriers in northwestern Europe. Library Archives Canada

▼ A Conger mine clearing device mounted on a Carrier hull (probably a Mortar Carrier MK I) towed by a Churchill AVRE (Armoured Vehicle Royal Engineers). The first Conger MK Is reached the European theatre of operations in September 1944. Private collection

▲ The armoured body of the Praying Mantis could be elevated to fire over obstacles. This strange vehicle was never tested in combat. Private collection

▼ The Praying Mantis in travelling position. Both Bren light machine guns could be removed from the turret by crew members. Author's collection

▲ A MK I Universal fitted with carpet laying equipment. Thanks to this particular device, a roll of hessian mat was un-wounded over obstacles like barbed wire or muddy ground as the vehicle moved forward, permitting the advance of friendly infantry. The Carrier illustrated here shows an empty spool. Private collection

▼ The 'Tugboat' was an experimental vehicle based on the T16 MK I. It was designed to counteract anti-personnel mines laid to avoid anti-tank minefields clearance. To lower ground pressure, it was equipped with four tracks and their corresponding suspension bogies, idlers and sprockets. Library Archives Canada

▲ One of the three Armoured Snowmobile MK Is received by Soviet Union. This two-man reconnaissance tracked vehicle was able to cross all kinds of snowy, muddy and sandy grounds. The Snowmobile was tested by the 5th Canadian Armoured Brigade in Italy, at the beginning of 1945. Private collection

▼ A Carrier, Tracked, CT20 (also known as Carrier, Oxford MK I) towing a 17 pdr anti-tank gun. The CT 20, considered the last of the line of British Carriers, was tested at the end of the war as a gun tractor and a 3in Mortar Carrier. Germany, exact date unknown. Library Archives Canada

BIBLIOGRAPHY

BOOKS

- Brojo P., *"Loyd Carrier MK I/MK II"*, Capricorn Publications, 2014.

- Chamberlain P., D. Crow, *"Carriers"*, Profile Publications Ltd., 1970.

- Chamberlain P., C. Ellis, "Making Tracks – British Carrier Story, 1914 to 1972", Profile Publications Ltd., 1973

- Fletcher D., *"Universal Carrier 1936-48, The Bren Gun Carrier Story"*, Osprey Publishing Ltd., 2005.

- Icks R., *"Carden Loyd MK. VI"*, Profile Publications Ltd., 1967.

- Pignato N., *"Le cingolette dell'E.I. - L'Universal in Italia"*, Centro Ricerche Storiche, 2008 [PDF].

- Watson N., *"Universal Carriers – Vol. 1"*, Nigel Watson, 2007.

- Watson N., *"Universal Carriers – Vol. 2"*, Nigel Watson, 2008.

- Watson N., *"Universal Carriers – Vol. 3"*, Nigel Watson, 2011.

MILITARY MANUALS

- Mechanization Pamphlet No. 7, Australian Military Forces, *"Carriers, Machine Gun LP., Nos. 2&2A – Description, Operation And Maintenance"*, Automotive Engineering Panel, Ministry Of Munitions, 1941

- *"Carriers: Service Instruction Book"*, Chilwell Catalogue No 63/63, 1944.

- *"Carrier Universal MK I* and MK II* - Illustrated Parts Catalogue 1941-4"*, Ford Motor Company of Canada Ltd., 1944.

- *"Loyd Carriers: Service Instruction Books"*, Chilwell Catalogue No. 63/68, 1944.

- Technical Manual 9-746 *"Universal Carrier T16"*, War Department, 11 August 1943.

TITOLI PUBBLICATI - ALREADY PUBLISHING

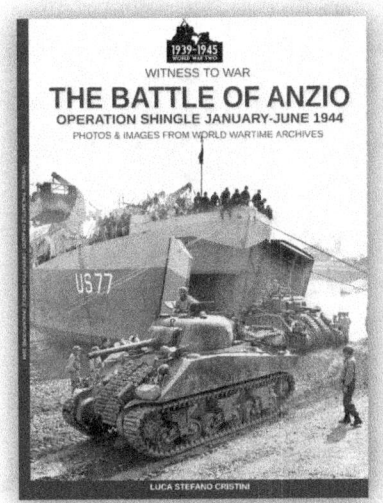

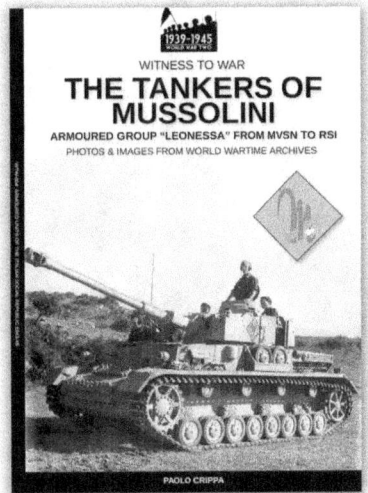

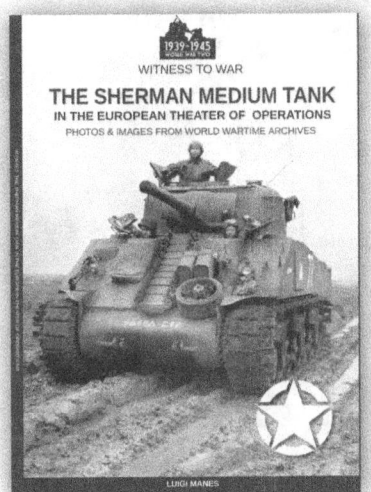

BOOKS TO COLLECT